Deconstruction / Reconstruction

Conversations at the Dusty Thistle

A STORY OF THE GEN Z GENERATION
STANDING AT THE CROSSROADS OF FAITH

By Tri Robinson

Copyright © 2025 by Tri Robinson

All rights reserved. No part of this book may be reproduced in any form or by any electronic or mechanical means including information storage and retrieval systems without written permission from the publisher, except for a reviewer who may quote brief passages in a review.

Published by Timber Butte Publishing, Sweet, Idaho
ISBN: 978-1-7370315-3-6

Printed in the United States of America. First Edition. All rights reserved under international copyright law. Contents and/or cover may not be reproduced in whole or in part in any form without the express written consent of the publisher.

A Dedication

I want to dedicate this story to the hundreds of youth leaders across America. My story is not about youth who attend vibrant and meaningful high school-age youth groups connected to healthy Christian churches, but rather those no longer under parental authority: college-age, 20s, and thirties. Youth leaders are often the last line of influence for teens, who will soon make their own adult decisions concerning what they believe, who they want to become as adults, and the values that will guide them. My hat goes off to the men and women who have taken the challenge to engage with teen youth, and I pray God will fill them with wisdom, energy, and vision.

Deconstruction / Reconstruction
An explanation

Statistics tell us that the Christian church has been losing a million Gen Zs and Millennials every year. In the not-too-distant future, this phenomenon will become the demise of American Evangelicalism on two accounts: at one end, the grandchildren of Boomers are falling away from churches across America by the thousands, while on the other end, the Boomers are beginning to die off rapidly. American Evangelicals are happy now because, in their mind, they have gained victory by achieving power and political control, but their satisfaction may well be short-lived. Let me explain.

In the late 1980s, the American church experienced a shift as the excitement from the Jesus Movement of the 1970s began to fade. The Baby Boomers, who were recognized for their radical behavior in the 1960s, started to lose their enthusiasm for change and began pursuing the great American dream of wealth and power. By the mid-1990s, the Christian church had become infiltrated with a new message, initially subtle but unapologetic. The Moral Majority believed that the church should control national and local politics, and this message/agenda seriously impacted the Body of Christ. This has now become known as "Christian Nationalism." This would rapidly undermine the true ministry of Jesus in the church as it chose politics over authentic faith. While many Christians drank the poison, believing this political agenda was the will of God, they didn't realize the collateral damage this course of action would have. That is, their children rejected the poison but, in so doing, also rejected the church, which they perceived as being the root of the problem.

The word "deconstruction" has many interpretations. Still, most Christian sociologists have concluded that it speaks of people, primarily young people, who have rejected their faith in search of new spiritual truths. Most often, that truth results from both hunger and disillusionment and is contrived through human reasoning.

This short narrative, "Deconstruction / Reconstruction," is fictitious but tells of an actual reality. It reflects the hearts of a young generation hungry for spiritual truth but who have given up on finding it in the established church. For those who have come upon this story whose adult children no longer attend church, or for church leaders who care why this phenomenon is so prevalent, this short story is for you. My motive for telling this story, which takes place in a quaint, hidden away mountain tavern, is to encourage two groups of people: parents who have experienced the heartbreak of seeing their children or grandchildren reject the church and also pastors and leaders who are willing to open their eyes to the crisis. I am in both camps, and I pray what you are about to read will stir a hunger to understand the heart of the problem.

Table of Contents

Chapter 1 – Sara's Pain

Chapter 2 – First Encounter at the Dusty Thistle

Chapter 3 – The Horse Before the Cart

Chapter 4 – The Red Letters

Chapter 5 – Traffic Patterns

Chapter 6 – New Lights

Chapter 7 – Roots of Anxiety

Chapter 8 – A Flicker of Light

Chapter 9 – Encounter

Chapter 10 – A Turning Point

Chapter 11 – What Is It You Want?

Chapter 12 – Deconstruction? / Reconstruction?

Chapter 1 – Sara's Pain

"I'm done!" Sara said emphatically. "I mean, I'm really done."

She restated it the second time with a softer tone of sorrow in her voice. Tears welled in her eyes as she said it, and I'll admit, in mine as well.

I felt for her. Sara was a good girl, a wonderful person, and I knew that.

"What are you going to do now?" I asked, knowing she had come to the end of her rope.

Sara was 27 years old. She was a "tweener," either the last of the millennials or the start of the Gen Z group. In either case, what she told me is indicative of both designated social groups. I knew that many people in these generations felt the same way because, for whatever reason, they had felt safe talking about it with my wife, Nancy, and me.

"I'm not giving up on Jesus," she said, "I just don't get church. Somehow, it doesn't feel relevant to me anymore. Every Sunday morning is the same; it's been the same for as long as I can remember. Not only is the message not targeted at my generation, but so much is said that doesn't feel real or even right regarding our present-day culture. Maybe it's just too black and white in a world that's chaotic and out of control."

I sat and listened. The truth was, I wanted to understand her perspective. I'd been hearing similar complaints from younger people for quite a while. I genuinely wanted to understand because most of my adult life had been dedicated to making the "church" a healthy, relevant place. Also, I'd learned that being defensive or argumentative with her generation was fruitless.

"What happened?" I asked Sara. "Why is your conviction to leave your church coming to a head now?"

Sara had come from a congregation of about two hundred people. I didn't know much about it, but I did know it had recently gone through some difficult times. People were leaving, and most of them were younger. I also knew what Sara was experiencing was not uncommon to her generation. First, Millennials and then Gen Zs were making a mass exodus from organized religion across America and in other countries like the UK. During the 2020s, according to the Barna Research report, nearly half of Millennials either dropped out of church or became church hoppers. It seemed as if there was a plague of discontent. I truly wanted to understand.

Sara told me her story. "People are mean," she said. "Our pastor tried hard not to share his honest political convictions, but he couldn't help it."

I knew what she shared was true; it was a dilemma for nearly everyone. If pastors wanted to teach the Bible with sincerity and truth, it would be almost impossible not to let their feelings concerning the political climate leak out. Everyone was so divided, and no matter what they said, someone would be upset.

"What I discovered," she continued, "was that people's political convictions carry more weight than their stated religious beliefs. It seems like a person's theology should be congruent with their ideology, but I found that wasn't the case."

Wow! I had to think about that. I must admit it was an interesting analysis on her part. Most everyone understands what a theological position is. Many churches sing the Doxology or recite a statement of faith almost every Sunday. Ideology, on the other hand, is a more profound thing. Ideology is what forms the identity of a person. In some regards, it overrides theology because it deals with the whole belief system of a person in and out of their church life. In a sense, it's what a person believes about the world around them and what they truly value. We can fake our theological views, proclaiming religious beliefs about who God is and what He wants of us, but we can't hide from our ideology because it drives our very character and actions. It motivates, for example, how we vote.

"Well, that's an interesting thought, Sara," I said after what probably seemed to her like a long pause of thinking on my part. "What happens," I asked, "if someone's theology and ideology conflict?"

Sara didn't pause but immediately spoke with passion in her voice. "Hypocrisy!" she blurted out. "They come off like hypocrites, and that's something our generation can't stomach. They say they believe in one thing but support just the opposite. They don't practice what they preach."

"Give me an example," I asked. I thought her reply was a bit overstated, but at the same time, I knew she was speaking out of pain. She was in the process of rejecting something she had held dear for most of her life.

"Okay," she came back. "I'll give you an example. Christian people say they believe in what Jesus commissioned His followers to do. Things like caring for the poor and embracing the immigrants, yet they whole-heartedly support the deportation of undocumented immigrants, even to the point of separating children from their parents. To me, that's not only unbiblical but outright criminal. It's flat-out wrong."

"We've got real problems on our southern border," I said. "People are afraid of the increase of drug and human trafficking. They're also afraid of losing job opportunities. Don't you think the politicians are just trying to bring law and order? Besides, they said they wouldn't separate families again."

"Not all those people are criminals," Sara said. "Thousands of people are bringing small children, some even on their backs. People don't walk a thousand miles for no reason. People are fleeing unbelievable conditions where they live. Yes, there's no question that something should be done about criminal activity. There's a need for law and order, but there's also a need for compassion. Besides, they separated families before, and if it wasn't for public opinion and pressure, I'm convinced they'd do it again." She looked right at me, her eyes filling with tears as they met mine. "You've been a pastor; don't you agree with me?"

"I do," I said with some regret for being the devil's advocate. "I know you're right, but somehow, politicians' legislation should consider and separate both scenarios, don't you think?"

"That's the trouble with laws," she said. "They're too often so black and white they don't consider their full ramification on people they may not even be intended for. Sometimes, they seem to lack logic or even common sense. I know we need laws, but they must be made with wisdom and hearts of compassion. Evicting illegal immigrants who sincerely need our compassion to punish the evildoers isn't right. It isn't the

Christ-like thing to do, and I think much of what's happening must be breaking the heart of Jesus – at least the Jesus I know and follow."

I knew she had a point, but I wanted to understand what she was really saying, especially regarding her idea of legalism. I asked her for more clarity.

Sara responded, "As I read the "red letters" of the Bible, the things Jesus said, I saw Him despising the Pharisees because they believed legalism was the only way they could control people and change their culture." There was a thoughtful pause before she spoke, and her voice softened. "It was as if the Kingdom of God, prayer, and the preaching of salvation weren't enough. It was as if God needed man's wisdom and help to make his plan work."

"Jesus said he didn't come to abolish the law but to fulfill it," I interjected.

"Yes," she said, "but not how the Pharisees did it. Jesus called them hypocrites, too. He proclaimed the law would be fulfilled by the coming of His Kingdom and ultimately by changing people's hearts. He would do it through godly justice driven by compassion and mercy. Black and white legalism may work in a human court of law, but not in God's Kingdom."

I loved what she said, and it resonated with my heart. "You're right, Sara," I admitted. "There's no question; Jesus really is the only way things can begin to heal our society. More one-sided legislation won't do that. It'll only drive our country further apart." Then I asked, "So what are you going to do?"

"I don't know," she said, "but I want to be around people who feel like I feel. People who will keep the message of Jesus central but who aren't afraid to speak freely about the real world and its many challenges. I want authenticity and honesty. I want to talk about applying the simple truth to our crises without political stigma and ideology messing up the conversation. I want to be around people who can see it. To be honest," she admitted, "I'm afraid. I'm afraid of things like climate change, the escalation of violence and hatred in the world, and a very uncertain future." Then, the tears became a torrent.

"Do you think you are alone?" I asked. "Do you know others that feel like you do?"

"I do," she said, wiping her eyes, seemingly embarrassed by her emotion. "I know many people my age who want to talk like we are doing right now. They don't want or need to be corrected. They'd like to be around people they perceive as non-religious but who still want a relationship with Jesus. Understand me, they want their thinking challenged, but they don't like to feel like they're being preached at."

"It gives me a sense of privilege knowing you have been willing to share all this with me," I spoke. "And, if you'd like, I'd love to participate with a group of your friends if they wouldn't see me as part of the problem." I paused, let my words sink in, and added, "How about if we make a date?"

Sara considered it briefly and then said, "It can't feel religious. It would be best if it were not at a church."

"I get it," I said. "I know a good place, but the gathering would have to be small. Say, not more than a half dozen people."

"I totally agree," she came back, "but where?"

"I have a friend who lives on a nearby ranch. It's a historical place; for some reason, he has converted one of his old outbuildings into a classic pub-like place. It's not public; in fact, it's been sort of a secret kept for our small community up here. He calls it the 'Dusty Thistle.' I think he'd be more than happy to host something like this."

"It sounds perfect." Sara said. "When can we do it?"

"I'll tell you what," I responded, "you do the invite, and I'll ask my neighbor. Then you tell me about the best time for you."

"It's a date." she replied. "Tell your friend we promise to keep the Dusty Thistle a secret."

Chapter 2 – First Encounter at the Dusty Thistle

My wife Nancy and I drove slowly down the gravel road toward our neighbor's ranch. It was a moonless, snowy night, and I thought about Sara's friends who would be trying to find the entrance gate in the dark. We hoped the two or three inches of snow wouldn't discourage them from coming.

I'd been a pastor, church leader, Christian speaker, and author for most of my adult life. I had preached to hundreds and, at times, thousands of people in my long career, but thinking about my first meeting at the Dusty Thistle gave me pause. This was an altogether new thing for both Nancy and me. We suspect that these young adults might be wary of us. They were coming because the church had disillusioned them, and we probably represented the establishment they had rejected. It was a risk, but then, we had taken many risks in our 55 years of marriage for the sake of God's Kingdom. We felt this meeting at the Dusty Thistle would be worth the risk. Besides that, the shoe was now on the other foot. Many years before, there had been a time when we were in their place. In the 1960s, we, too, rejected the traditional churches of our parents, but unlike them, we rediscovered faith amid the phenomenon known as the "Jesus Movement." If we could in some way help them discover what we have found, it would be worth everything.

We drove through our neighbor Brad's front gate and then a second gate that led to a collection of rustic cabins and sheds. Sara's car and another were parked in front of a large, unremarkable outbuilding. Over the door was a carved sign with jagged ends that read 'The Dusty Thistle'.

"I see you guys found this place," I remarked as Nancy and I entered the unique but familiar room. The Dusty Thistle had two large wood-burning parlor stoves at each end of the room. It was the sole means of heat in the place, and the young people quickly discovered how to take the chill off the otherwise drafty room by putting their backs to the stove. The Dusty Thistle had an ambiance of something from the past. They also discovered that The Dusty Thistle was in the shadow of a mountain, which restricted the use of cell phones.

"We did." one of the boys said. "It wasn't easy; in fact, it was a little scary not knowing if we were in the right place." There was uncertainty in his voice, and his demeanor made me fight back an urge to laugh.

Looking across an old wooden bar lit with antique beer signs and classic overhead tavern lighting, our friend Brad was unsuccessfully trying to hide a mischievous smile. I could tell he was enjoying their uneasiness, which made me laugh.

Nancy was the first to speak. She spotted Sara, who gave her a warm smile. "Hi, Sara," she began with an upbeat voice. "Please introduce us to your friends." Without waiting for Sara's response, she grabbed the hand of the boy closest to her and said, "Hi, my name is Nancy. How wonderful you guys were willing to make such a long trip to get here on this dark night."

They had driven over an hour to get there: over a mountain pass, along a river, across an old iron trestle bridge, and up a narrow, winding, unsurfaced road for the better part of eight miles. It seemed like a long venture for people who hadn't been there before.

Nancy and I went one-by-one, shaking the hands of the half dozen young people, hoping to make them feel welcome and at home. Brad welcomed them by offering them drinks from his classic old bar, which may have thrown them further off balance. I'm sure they'd never been to any religious event where they were offered free drinks ranging from water to soft drinks to imported beer to Kentucky bourbon. The Dusty Thistle itself was an experience. Brad is a collector of classic memorabilia, and he used his years of collecting to decorate what had been a drafty ranch machine shop into a tavern with the ambiance of a 1930s or '40s pub.

"What are our options?" one of the boys questioned.

That's where I made my first mistake. Without thinking, I spontaneously sang the first stanza of an old '60s Arlo Guthrie song, "You can get anything you want at Alice's restaurant . . ." Then, to make things worse, Brad finished the line by singing, "Except Alice." Everything went quiet for a minute, and it dawned on me that we were singing to the wrong generation. I'm sure most of them had never heard of Arlo Guthrie, much less "Alice's Restaurant." They politely laughed but more at us than with us. It struck me that maybe I wasn't the guy for this job. Perhaps I was just too old, from a different generation, but to them, maybe from a different planet.

"Let's have a seat." I suggested. "Why don't we grab some chairs or barstools and sit around the front of the stove."

After we were all seated, I continued, "I know, because of my conversations with Sara, that most of you are struggling with your Christian faith. Because of that, Nancy and I volunteered to be listening ears. Early on in our lives, we struggled with the same thing. We believe what you're going through is a healthy and normal part of an authentic faith journey."

I didn't want to sound preachy or dominate the moment, so I became quiet. I hadn't asked a question that begged for an answer; I had just stated what I believed to be the obvious. The room became silent.

After what seemed to be a long, awkward pause, a guy named Eric spoke up. "Honestly," he said, "I'm not sure what I feel. I know I've not just become disillusioned with church life but have found myself becoming angry. I guess I've had questions that nobody seems to be able to answer." Several others nodded in agreement.

Eric seemed to be a thoughtful young man. We didn't know until later that Eric had a good reason for his confusion and disillusionment. Like most of these young people, he had a backstory for questioning his faith and for his underlying anger. Several years before, Eric had lost a close friend in a mass school shooting. The craziness of the world had directly impacted his life.

"What kind of questions?" I asked.

Eric seemed embarrassed to go further, but a girl named Elaine, sitting to his left, answered for him. "Like, where is God in this out-of-control world? So many of our friends are either apathetic, saying nothing really matters anymore, or they're acting out their anger or fear. Everyone is messed up and confused, and the church seems to be playing it safe, trying not to offend anyone in such a polarized time. We want direction and real truth when everyone seems to make up their own truth. It isn't easy to sort things out, never knowing who and what to believe."

Like many of those who met at The Dusty Thistle that night, Elaine had been raised in an Evangelical church and was a thinker and a good communicator. Somewhere along the line, something motivated her to question many of the ideals she was taught. Like many of the group, she was not timid when expressing her issues.

"What is truth, anyway?" a guy named Shannon asked scornfully.

I was surprised to observe how the idea of truth struck a nerve. It made me realize the questions they were asking were questions every Christian should be asking, especially when it came to the concept of truth. Jesus proclaimed more than once that He was the truth, and I wondered how many people ever really contemplated His claim. Jesus said He was the truth, and the truth would set us free. When Jesus was on trial before Pontius Pilate in John 18:37, Pilate asked Jesus if He was a King, and Jesus replied, "You say that I am a king. In fact, the reason I was born and came into the world is to testify to the truth. Everyone on the side of truth listens to me." Then Pilate retorted, "What is truth?" In my mind, he probably said it with sarcasm the way Shannon did.

"I'd say truth is pretty central to the Christian faith," Eric interjected. "In today's world, truth seems to be lost or at least covered over by so many mistruths, if not outright lies."

Eric's comments broke things open; everyone in the room had strong opinions on the subject. Comments bounced around the circle, many being stated with emotion and feeling. We talked about why truth has seemingly lost its way in our society. They spoke of the internet, social media, and the rapid advance in AI. Most of them had abandoned televised news, saying it was nothing more than opinion and unvetted biased commentary. They spoke of how it had become America's new entertainment and addicting to their parents' generation. They confessed how "the news" depressed and frightened them and expressed why most of their generation had opted to turn to the internet, or cellphone feeds to get their sound bite information. They couldn't understand how or why so many of the Christian community had bought into the extreme right-wing conspiracy theories when they were not only bogus but dangerous. Their honesty enlightened Nancy and me and led me to ask, "Do you guys understand the difference between absolute and relative truth?"

The Dusty Thistle had warmed up some as Brad had been stoking the two parlor stoves with chunks of hard, dry wood, and then coats, one by one, started to come off, exposing tattoos on the arms of a few of the group. Shannon was a taller young man with shoulder-length hair. I glanced at his tattooed arms, trying to see if they would give any hint of his ideological thinking as so many tattoos do. They didn't, but his comments had come out more strongly than others. To me, he seemed to have some underlying pain. "Well," he said again, with an attitude, "why don't you tell us? What's the difference?"

By the tone of his voice, I thought maybe he had some issue with authority and that he most likely perceived Nancy and me as a sign of that authority because we were so much older. I carefully responded, "I'm only here, Shannon, as a participant because we were asked to be by Sara."

"I'm sorry," he came back. "It's just that this conversation is pushing my buttons. It bothers me that people can't see what we are seeing. To be honest, any religious conversation really bothers me."

Paul intervened, "I guess it's not rocket science. Absolute truth is what is true. It's substantiated truth. When Jesus said He was the truth, He spoke of authentic, verified truth. Relative truth, on the other hand, is not absolute. It's based on bias and individual perception. It's like saying your truth may not be my truth. We both may have our own belief systems because of our different world views, but if that's the case, then there is no absolute truth. If there's no absolute truth, then there's no truth at all. I don't know if I'm making sense, but that's how I understand it."

"What did Jesus mean when He said He was the way, the truth, and the life?" Elaine asked.

Her asking that question made me realize that these guys were not biblically illiterate; in fact, I learned that all of them came from what would be called Evangelical churches and families. I waited, resisting the urge to jump in with answers. I was trying hard not to open my mouth, but I was impressed by her interjecting such a pertinent verse. I realized that most of these young folks weren't mindlessly questioning their Christian faith.

"I was taught the 'way,' was Jesus' way, which was love," Angie, another one of the girls, spoke up. "And when people live His way, the truth breaks into their lives, leading to a full and meaningful life. It happens in that order: the way, the truth, and the life."

Angie looked at Nancy and me, hoping for affirmation. She was right in what she said, but I wondered if she truly believed it and could apply it to her life. I hoped so. These were good kids, and Nancy and I felt a sense of privilege to have been allowed to participate. As the conversation continued into the evening, I realized they didn't have huge issues with Jesus and His ministry; something else had turned them off to a life of Christianity.

It was getting late, and the six had to return to the city. We observed that not one of them had abused the open bar. In fact, the two who would be driving home had avoided alcohol altogether. We said how much we loved meeting them and how valuable their insights had been for us. We invited all of them to rejoin us and continue the conversation. They thanked us and promised to return, asking if they could bring some other friends. We agreed and set a date.

Brad, who mostly stayed behind the bar except for stoking fires and serving refreshments, later told us how much the conversation had meant to him and assured us that The Dusty Thistle would always be available.

Chapter 3 – The Horse Before the Cart

It was the usual way we started almost every winter morning, living the way we did after having been retired for so many years. I'd get up just before dawn with Wolfie and Sadie, our two dogs, and start a fire in the living room stove. I'd let the dogs out, get dressed, and make coffee. Then, I'd pull on my farm boots and head out to feed the livestock: the horses, cows, sheep, and chickens. After checking that everyone's water was ice-free, I'd return to the living room with a fresh armload of firewood.

The room was already getting cozy when Nancy made her entrance. Watching her look into the flames of the fire I had just built, I was motivated to break into another old song. I sang the first stanza of the Waylon Jennings ballad, "Put another log on the fire – Cook me up some bacon and some beans . . ." then kiddingly reminded her it was a woman's work to build fires. It might have been early for such fun, but she quickly responded, "I'm so glad you're finally getting in touch with your feminine side."

With that, we poured coffee and sat on the sofa, looking into the crackling flames together. It had become our practice to listen to a short online devotional first thing each day, getting our eyes on the Lord before the tasks of the day stole our minds away.

The morning after our experience at The Dusty Thistle, we couldn't help reflecting on the conversation we had witnessed. "You know," Nancy spoke with empathy, "what those kids need more than anything else is an authentic experience with the Holy Spirit as we had. They need a revelation of Jesus for themselves. I think they have focused more on the church than on a Christ-centered relationship. I believe if they pursued Jesus by way of authentic revelation, their church life would follow."

"I know what you're saying," I replied. "We can talk, talk, talk, attempting to help them sort all this church stuff out, but the only thing that will change anything is a fresh revelation of God's existence and Jesus' love for them. You're also right, saying it was the thing that changed us in the beginning. At the same time, there is a lot of confusion to sort out these days, and I still have empathy for that."

Nancy's comments got me thinking. I recalled various times and events during our earlier days of learning what it meant to walk with God. Both of us had what we considered supernatural experiences. Those experiences occurred because of our hunger to know God better and to understand what He wanted for our lives. We lived with a kind of expectancy that He could speak to us in multiple ways, not just through theological concepts.

"I was remembering," she recalled, "most of the major decisions we've made in our lives have resulted from trying to discern God's voice. On the flip side, because of our involvement in the early days of the Jesus Movement, we tended to see scripture as being very black and white."

In our insecurity, we relied on what we were taught by young pastors who tended to be legalistic. But after years of reading and studying the Bible, we realized some serious issues with that early training, seeing some inconsistencies between the New Testament and the Old Testament and from one biblical author to another.

"It kind of gives you compassion for these young people," Nancy continued. "Learning what we have over the years, I can feel their pain when it comes to perceiving discrepancies in what they have been taught about scripture. They need to learn how to read scripture through the filter of the red letters, the actual words of Jesus. They honestly need a revelation of His reality in their hearts before it makes sense in their minds."

"It's like the horse and the cart analogy," I finished her thought. "Like so many, their reliance on truth depends more on a church experience than an encounter with Jesus Himself. The cart has gone before the horse."

"Do you remember all those years ago when you and I were brand new Christians?" Nancy asked. "Your dad told us there were many mysteries regarding the Bible and the Christian experience. Because we had been so wrapped up in the Jesus Movement mentality, we believed Christianity was cut and dry, and there was no mystery."

I laughed out loud. "We really did have all the truth in those days, didn't we? We believed when it came to salvation, you were either in or out. If you turned to Christ by repeating a simple prayer, you would avoid burning in Hell. We called it jokingly, 'Turn or burn theology.' To us, there were no mysteries because the Bible told us everything we needed to know."

She laughed with me, "Your dad explained that if there were no mysteries, there would be no need for faith. It took us a long time to fully comprehend what he said."

I agreed, "In the Christian faith, there is plenty of mystery, and the older I get, the more comfortable I am responding to many theological questions by saying simply, 'I just don't know.'"

"I guess we've had to learn, sometimes, the hard way," she added, "coming to Christ and learning to trust and follow Him is a process. It's a process not everyone is willing to pursue diligently. I think some people start a faith journey but become overwhelmed with life, while others become enamored by the lure of security, wealth, and power. They either give up on a life of faith or become Christian in name only."

"Others," I finished her thought, "like the young people we are meeting with at The Dusty Thistle, who had found some level of faith but struggled to make it fully their own. It seems to me that most of them desire a relationship with God, but because they equate their relationship with the church as a central part of their relationship with God, they are now on the verge of throwing the baby out with the bath water. The thing they needed, as you had said, is a revelation of Christ. The church would then become important because it would gather those who had truly discovered what they had in Christ."

"Yes," she agreed, "the church would become an authentic community of Christ followers. It would be a place to grow and learn, a place to receive ministry, prayer, and support, a place to be encouraged, and a place to serve. It would be a place willing to live in mystery yet grasp an expectation for eternity. The church would be a place to live out a life of growing faith with other like-hearted and like-minded people. That is, if it was an actual Christ-centered body of believers who were together in pursuit of the pure and simple truth of the gospel. As you said, Jesus would be the horse, and the church would be the cart to help carry them through life. Maybe it's our job to help them rediscover the value of such a place."

Chapter 4 – The Red Letters

"Some people have been telling me I've been in the process of deconstruction," Alicia said with a look of confusion. "Could you tell me what that is? Do you think that's what I'm doing?" It was our second meeting at The Dusty Thistle. Alicia was another of Sara's original friends. Our circle of six had grown to eight since our last gathering.

"Alicia," I said, "I don't know you well, but what I do know of you is that you're a sensitive, thoughtful girl. I've heard you say you've been disappointed and hurt by your church experience. I think you're going through an evaluation of church life more than wanting to challenge scripture or the tenets of your faith. As I understand it, deconstruction is rethinking scripture and faith altogether. It speaks of searching for forms of spirituality outside of the

Christian faith. From what I've heard and seen, I don't think that's you."

"Maybe it's me," Shannon jumped in. "I have major issues with scripture. I read about all the violence in the Old Testament, the attitude towards the LGBTQ community, and even the roles of women in the New Testament, and it feels like what the Bible says is totally out of date with the real world, at least the world we're living in. I've kind of had it with the whole human race. I came to Jesus because I thought He was supposed to usher in a new way of thinking and living. A kinder way."

"And you're right," I came back. "Jesus did. If you read the entire Bible through the lens of His spoken words, I think you might see things a little more clearly regarding the Christian faith." I came off sounding more preachy than I wished, and even as I said it, I wanted to kick myself. "I'm sorry, Shannon," I said. "These subjects aren't all black and white, and in many cases, there's no easy answers."

Shannon lifted a hand and mildly apologized. We all realized there were strong feelings in the air. The conversations we were engaging in were starting to enter some difficult territory, and I realized, maybe too late, that they were a bigger deal than any of us fully realized.

"What about homosexuality?" Angie jumped in. Angie was another of the original group. "I know people who are a part of the gay community. Most of them were clearly born with homosexual tendencies. God made them the way they are. Does the Bible say they are doomed to hell? I can't buy that even if it's what the Bible says."

"Angie, I can tell you what I believe the Bible says about it, but you may not be able to agree fully with everything I say."

"Go ahead and tell us," Angie responded. "We all want to know what you think and where you stand."

I realized everyone there wanted, maybe even needed, to know. In a way, I felt like I was on trial, and if convicted guilty, this whole experimental conversation would be finished. I also realized everyone there had at least one friend who fell into this category, and they had empathy for them. They had seen what they perceived to be harshness on the part of the Evangelical churches they had been a part of, and it was one more thing that made them question their faith. I was walking on thin ice.

"Before I start," I said, "there are some Bibles called *Red Letter Editions*. Every word Jesus speaks in those manuscripts is printed in red. Throughout the letters of the Apostles, anytime Jesus is quoted, His words are also printed in red. That's why I've been saying, as followers of Christ, we need to read the entire Bible through the lens of the red letters."

I continued, "One of the hardest statements in the New Testament is found in the first chapter of Paul's letter to the Romans. Let's read it before we continue this discussion." I looked around the circle, wondering if anyone had brought a Bible. Sara, who was clearly emerging as the group leader, raised her hand. To everyone's surprise, she pulled her Bible out of a large bag she carried as a purse. She began reading verse 24.

24 Therefore God gave them over in the sinful desires of their hearts to sexual impurity for the degrading of their bodies with one another. 25 They exchanged the truth about God for a lie and worshiped and served created things rather than the Creator—who is forever praised. Amen.

26 Because of this, God gave them over to shameful lusts. Even their women exchanged natural sexual relations for unnatural ones. 27 In the same way the men also abandoned natural relations with women and were inflamed with lust for one another. Men committed shameful acts with other men, and received in themselves the due penalty for their error.

28 Furthermore, just as they did not think it worthwhile to retain the knowledge of God, so God gave them over to a depraved mind, so that they do what ought not to be done. 29 They have become filled with every kind of wickedness, evil, greed and depravity. They are full of envy, murder, strife, deceit and malice. They are gossips, 30 slanderers, God-haters, insolent, arrogant and boastful; they invent ways of doing evil; they disobey their parents; 31 they have no understanding, no fidelity, no love, no mercy. 32 Although they know God's righteous decree that those who do such things deserve death, they not only continue to do these very things but also approve of those who practice them.

When Sara had finished, the room was silent until Shannon broke the silence by speaking under his breath, "That's a bunch of crap. That's crazy stuff!"

I wasn't sure what he meant by "crazy stuff," so I let the silence take effect, waiting for more reaction. The next comment came from Angie. "What does that even mean?" she asked.

Her tone wasn't one of anger but one of hurt and confusion.

"That's why I wanted you to hear it for yourselves," I spoke. "Paul is not talking about homosexuality alone, but about all kinds of sin. It's envy, strife, deceit, gossip, slander, rudeness, arrogance, boastfulness, lack of faithfulness, not loving, no mercy, even being disobedient to parents. Homosexuality is just one thing thrown into a huge pile of unrighteous behavior. As you guys know, the Bible calls those behaviors sin."

"Let me ask you one question," I added, "who here is without sin? And, if sin separates us from God, who here will make it to heaven without His intervention?" I paused and let that much sink in before adding, "We are all held captive to sin of any and every kind, and in my mind, we're all guilty; I know I am."

Again, everyone was silent, even Shannon, who didn't have a quick response. "But we are talking about homosexuality," Angie reminded me.

"Yes," I said, "but my point is, it can't be isolated as a greater sin than all the rest; at least, I don't think it was in Paul's mind. Sin is sin, and all of us are somewhere in that pile at one time or another."

"What are you saying?" Eric asked. "As far as I know, Jesus never even mentioned it. Instead, He hung out with tax collectors and sinners."

"You're right about that," I responded. "I'm only saying that we all need to receive God's grace to get through this life. We need His intervention and His provision for forgiveness. I'm saying we can't talk about homosexuality as if it is a stand-alone sin. We can't talk about it without looking at our own lives first. I'm saying the entire human race needs the provision of grace and God's forgiveness. It's kind of like the red letters again, where Jesus said to the Pharisees, "You look at the sliver in your neighbor's eye but can't see the log in your own eye."

"But, specifically," Eric said, "if a gay person falls in love and marries another gay person, and they authentically love each other and adopt a baby and live happily ever after, will they go to hell?"

That's when I remembered my father's words: "You've got to learn to live in the mystery. You've got to realize there are some things you'll never know for sure until you're face to face with Jesus. Certainty is the enemy of faith. If there were no mystery, there would be no need for faith."

"Eric," I said with humility, "there are some things I'll have to admit, I just don't know."

Chapter 5 – Traffic Patterns

Another two weeks had passed, and our small group was again gathering around the old parlor stove at the Thistle. Because we had already gone through breaking the ice, learning names, and getting to know one another better, everyone had become more relaxed and social. The group seemed to be comfortable cozying up to the fire on what was still a chilly winter evening. They had also become familiar with the drive and less intimidated, not only by the back country roads but also by the uniqueness of Brad's country pub. Several of them brought food, and some brought hand-crafted beer to enhance Brad's hospitality. Nancy and I observed how they seemed more relaxed, talkative, and open. Walls were breaking down.

Paul was the first to speak that night. "I've been thinking," he began, "I didn't stop attending church because I was so mad or disillusioned like many of you guys, but these conversations have made me look at myself and evaluate my motives. Church was okay; I just got tired of going."

"Why's that?" someone asked.

"I don't know," he said. "Somehow, it just got old, a little boring, I guess. As I grew up, my priorities changed, and I moved on. I left home and lived in the dorm at the university, where I developed a whole new circle of friends who had more in common with me. Hardly any of them were church-goers. The church just worked its way out of my traffic pattern."

"How's that?" Leah asked. "What do you mean, your traffic pattern?"

"My life just changed," he replied. "I think one of the main reasons I went to church was for a relationship, but my new friends hung out in coffee houses or brew pubs. On the weekends, we went skiing in the winter and river rafting in the summer. My free time was filled up with stuff I loved doing. Not only that, but as a college student, I sit in lectures all week long, and the last thing I feel like doing on Sunday is sitting through another long lecture."

What Paul was saying struck me. Having been a pastor myself for so many years, I knew what he was saying made some sense. One of our primary responsibilities as pastors was to spend hours every week preparing messages, thinking it was our best means of conveying spiritual information to the throngs of people who gathered in our buildings week after week. It was what was expected of us as teachers. Maybe there was a different, better way, but for the life of me, I couldn't think of an alternative at that moment.

Before I entered the ministry, I was a junior high school teacher. I learned quickly in those days that if I didn't keep my classes interesting and captivating, my students would make me pay. I could continually evaluate how I was doing based on their behavior. People in the church don't generally throw spit wads at the clock if they get bored; junior high students do. I found the best way to keep them motivated was through participation. I discovered that true learning had to be done by kinetic means, that is, through physical hands-on activity. We called it experiential education. I think this same philosophy should be applied in the ministry.

I could look at those issues later, but at that moment, I was more fascinated by Paul's comment about traffic patterns.

"So, Paul, explain again what you mean by traffic patterns," I said. "That concept fascinates me."

Elaine interrupted, "It's like going to places where you feel the most comfortable, places that match your lifestyle. Starbucks or some other hangout where you can meet friends and talk without any agenda. I'm not in college right now, but I have a job, and I find myself gravitating to places like that with my coworkers and other friends." Elaine paused as if struggling with something. Then she said, "I don't know if Paul feels like I do, but even though I understand and agree with him, I fight guilt when I substitute my new active life instead of going to church."

"You'll get over it," Paul broke in. "It only takes a little practice to break the habit." Looking at Nancy and me, he continued, "Be honest, when you were our age, didn't you get tired of your old church life?"

"You're right," I admitted. "During our college days, we were just like you, but when the Jesus

Movement broke out, everything changed for us after that."

I could see the wheels turning in Nancy's head. Then she said, "The thing that drew us back to church was a young pastor who came to our small city after we had first married. His name was Brent. He was a creative guy and had been burned by his past church experience, just like so many of our generation had. Right from the get-go, he did things innovatively and unconventionally. He gathered a handful of young people who wanted to help him get a new church going, and together, they pooled their money and rented a small, abandoned storefront studio. They spent days working together, cleaning the building and painting the walls. They found a dumpster behind a carpet outlet and got permission to take all the rejected carpet samples, using them to cover the studio's concrete floor. None of the samples matched, but the funky mosaic look gave the place a unique character. One of the guys in his group was a welder, and in his garage, he welded table legs and constructed several dozen bistro tables. Together, they turned that little storefront into the coolest coffee house in the town. It was a magnet for our generation, and as you said, it became part of our traffic pattern."

"Yeah," I agreed, "we thought that place was the most "hip" place around. I'll never forget the first time Nancy and I went there. We sat around a table with some friends, drinking coffee. We listened to a young girl with long dark hair sitting on a stool on a small stage, playing the guitar and singing Christian songs unlike anything we had ever heard. She looked and sounded a lot like Joan Baez. The place was magical and matched our 1960s culture."

"That sure doesn't sound like any church I've ever been to," Eric said. "No wonder the Jesus Movement took off. Too bad there's not a place like that now."

The conversation changed then. I didn't realize it that evening, but when Nancy and I shared our first church experience, it only made them angrier. I realized they longed for something they didn't think existed. We knew in their hearts that they desired a deep spiritual experience that matched their culture but believed it was out of reach.

Nancy and I knew it wasn't a "cool" building that drew us into a life of service to Christ, but rather, it was an authentic encounter with the Spirit of God. Yet, at the same time, there was truth in the fact that the creative model that our first pastor, Brent, had made surely didn't hurt. It was one of the things that helped to draw us into a place where we could hear and receive the message for the first time. It also helped the church become part of our new traffic pattern.

Chapter 6– New Lights

"It truly pains me," I told Nancy one morning as we sat drinking coffee by the fire. "I know this group of kids are sincere. They wouldn't be making this trip up here every other week if they weren't really searching for answers, and it frustrates me feeling so inadequate when it comes to helping them."

"They're hurting," Nancy replied. "No question about that, but I don't think they are fully in touch with their feelings. One thing is for sure: they believe the church has let them down, and, in some cases, they equate the church with Jesus. It's hard for them to separate the two."

"Maybe we need to focus their eyes off the church and onto themselves," I said. "Maybe we could help them isolate the underlying things that are more of the real issues."

Nancy was quiet, probably trying to discern the issues, and then she asked me a question. "Do you remember that book you read in the 1980s that really fascinated you? It was about what constitutes revival. The author was a church historian who said certain things had always occurred in the culture before a spiritual awakening. I think the book was called *Mega Truth*."

"Oh yeah," I answered, "David McKenna. He was the guy who exposed me to the term "cultural disjuncture." I'll always remember that. He said five existing conditions or stages throughout church history were present and responsible for the birth of a spiritual awakening. I remember the first stage was underlying emotional stress, and the second was cultural disjuncture, a term I hadn't heard before."

"Go on," she said, "I think there may be something to this."

"Well," I said, trying to recall. "These five stages resulted from what he called a cultural parenthesis, which was also a new term to me then. A parenthesis is when the culture navigates the transition from one era to another. He wrote the book in the mid-80s, just as we transitioned from the Industrial Revolution to the Age of Information. At the time, computers were becoming accepted tools—ones everyone would soon own and depend on. Up until then, there was no internet, no cell phones, no email, no social media, and especially no artificial intelligence. All of that was purely science fiction stuff. Dick Tracy, the old comic book character, was the only one with a smartwatch in those days. It was all futuristic."

"I remember that like it was yesterday," Nancy laughed. "When you look back at it, for us, it all happened so fast, but to these young people, they never knew a world without it."

"An interesting thought," I said, "Our generation was the generation that witnessed the radical changes firsthand, but their children seem to be the greater recipients of the change. It's like secondary smoke."

"What do you mean?" she asked.

"You know," I went on, "when a person is a smoker, they have a good chance of getting cancer, but then those who live in a household of smokers, the ones who inhale the secondary smoke, can also get sick even though they never smoked. Maybe these kids are recipients of their parents' cultural stress."

"And it's still happening." I continued, "Think about AI. Talk about something catching society by surprise. It's scary to think about where that's headed. McKenna said that during a cultural shift such as that, people become off balance and uncomfortable because of such radical change. The world is shaken, causing social norms to be challenged and questioned. A time of parenthesis throws the culture off balance, with people not understanding the root of their stress. Everyone becomes bothered and insecure, and they look for things to blame. Even though the changes took place at the turn of the century, the ramifications of it have escalated and are still impacting our culture 20 or 30 years later."

"How about the five stages you mentioned before?" Nancy asked.

"The first stage was what he called *internal stress*," I continued. "People feel insecure about the changes but can't understand why they feel discomfort. Then comes the second stage, *cultural disjuncture*. In their discomfort, they begin blaming things and questioning everything, especially institutions like the government, the educational system, and, of course, the church. Disjuncture refers to a type of detachment from things—a separation from the things that once gave them a sense of belonging, comfort, and security. The bottom line is that things get bad before they can get good. As McKenna put it, awakenings always happen in troubled times."

"That's two things," she interjected. "What's the third, fourth, and fifth thing?"

"Actually," I said, "now that I think about it, if what McKenna is saying relates to the time we are presently experiencing, I believe we are in stage two – cultural disjuncture. That's why everything seems so out of control, frustrating, and confusing. The third stage is a *spiritual revival*, not an all-out spiritual awakening. It's an attempt to rescue lost values and truth. The Jesus Movement of the '70s was a revival but not an "Awakening." Awakenings impact huge geographical regions and could impact the entire world."

"The fourth stage, according to McKenna, is what he calls *prophetic voices*. These voices of authority begin calling people back to biblical standards and social justice or, more accurately, to the words of Jesus, what we've been calling the Red Letters. These voices will tell the new generation to filter out all the cultural noise and render things down to the authentic gospel. It's also the first flicker of revival because it gives young people hope and thus revives their spirits."

"The final stage is *renewal and reform*. When all five of these things occur, spiritual awakening may explode worldwide. It's like what Jesus spoke of in Matthew 24: "And this gospel of the kingdom will be preached in the whole world as a testimony to all nations…""

"What I forgot to say, however, was that historically, McKenna points out that Awakenings have always started with the emerging generation—young people who had experienced the same things our little group has been struggling with. McKenna called these young leaders 'New Lights.'"

"If we are presently experiencing a time of cultural disjuncture," Nancy spoke, "then why don't we ask our group of young folks what they are feeling, what's responsible for their stress?"

"That's a good idea," I said. "I've noticed people are starting to get honest lately. People are letting down their guards and allowing themselves to become more vulnerable. Honestly, I don't think it could have happened before now."

"Yeah," she agreed. "It's starting to feel safe, and that's precious. We need to protect what the Lord is doing among them. I doubt any of them will ever forget The Dusty Thistle."

What Nancy said reminded me of what had happened the previous week at the Thistle. We were engaged in discussions, sitting around one of the big parlor stoves. People were starting to open up, some for the first time, when the door opened, and one of our neighbors came in unannounced. It must have been awkward for him because, typically, the place was festive and full of laughter and life. The Dusty Thistle only opened on special occasions or events like the Super Bowl or the Kentucky Derby. When it was opened, it was filled with families and dogs and children. It was usually a place of celebration and joy, but what he now experienced was different. One of the girls who had been sharing her thoughts still had tears in her eyes. Brad was standing behind his bar as usual, and even though he wasn't an active participant in the group, he had been fully accepted and trusted. Hank, the neighbor who had popped in, got caught off guard and wasn't sure what to say. He seemed a little embarrassed.

"Howdy, everyone," he began. "Saw the lights were on and thought I'd see what's going on. Hope I didn't interrupt." Looking for comfort in an otherwise quiet room, he awkwardly said, "Hey Brad– just stopped to say hi."

Brad smiled, left the bar, and joined him at the back door. I'm not sure what he said, but he followed him out and probably tried to explain what we were all doing there. The point was that I realized then that we had become an intimate group where honesty and true feelings were accepted and safe. What we had was developing into something special—something worth protecting; you might say, something sacred.

Chapter 7 – Roots of Anxiety

The gentle sound of rain on the Thistle's aging, galvanized tin roof forced the group to gravitate into a closer circle than usual so that the quieter voices inside could be discerned. It was our sixth evening together, and inhibitions had lost their edge. There was an openness and freedom to be real, honest, and vulnerable. We had become a community with a purpose and a people with a shared cause. Everyone there had previous church experiences, but all had arrived at places of painful questioning, disillusionment, and frustration. They soon realized that the solutions would require more than simple explanations and pat answers. Some had thrown the Christian church out of their lives and, with it, their faith in the Lord. Their childhood belief system and Christian values were being laid out for the entire group to see, and the process was both challenging and painful. Everyone there was experiencing a bad case of spiritual disjuncture.

Nancy's and my job was not to fix them or even try but to help them navigate their way back to authentic truth.

Taking Nancy's lead from our previous discussion, I asked, "If you guys could define in one word what best describes your biggest struggle right now, what would it be?" It was a simple question, but it caused the room to go silent.

For a minute, I thought the meeting was over, as the void lasted way longer than usual. Then one of the girls, her name was Leah, blurted out, "I feel pissed! I feel ripped off! I feel angry, but I'm not sure why. I've blamed my anger on many valid things, but deep inside, I know they aren't the root cause."

"I guess we all feel a little that way, Leah," Sara interjected. "I've been having those feelings for a while, too, but I think I mostly feel fear, and I can't put my finger on why. I wake up at night feeling anxious – so much so that sometimes I think I'm losing my mind." Sara and Leah feebly covered their eyes to shield their tears from the rest of the group. There was silence again.

"Let's talk about fear for a minute," I suggested. Then, remembering McKenna's five stages, I said, "Anxiety is the root of most of our stress, and I guess if we were all honest, we'd have to admit we're feeling it."

"The world seems so uncertain right now," Paul spoke out. Paul was one of the newer guys in the group but a thoughtful person. There was kindness in him that made us all grateful for his presence. "There's a lot to be unsettled about, and what makes it scary is there seems to be no answers or solutions for much of it. It leaves me with an undefinable uneasiness. Sometimes, I become fatalistic about those things, feeling as if I want to check out or turn off my emotions or attitude of caring; it's all out of my control anyway."

What Paul communicated broke the room open. The echo of rain on the roof diminished as the room broke open with comments. As I sat there, I realized that the root cause of much of their anxiety and stress had been tapped into. The dam had broken.

"Apathy!" Shannon interjected. "I mean, who gives a damn if it's out of our control. It just is what it is. Screw it."

"Screw what?" I asked. "You guys are talking in hypotheticals – let's define what you are afraid of and what you can't change."

"The government, for one," Elaine spoke out. "Everyone tells us how much our vote counts, but with our electoral college voting system, a vote only counts if you live in a state that agrees with your viewpoint. I've long ago given up on politicians fixing anything. Everything is so polarized in America and has been most of our lives. Our generation doesn't even bother watching the news. Besides, most networks don't broadcast balanced or accurate news anyway. Most networks like Fox News and MSNBC are clearly biased. People turn on the station that best fits their worldview and political bias."

"Whenever I go home," Elaine continued, "my parents have Fox News on 24 hours a day, it seems like. I think they get brainwashed with all the negativities. I'll tell you for sure, what they watch on the news has a lot more influence on them than what they hear in church."

"And it seems like the church has bought into it, too," Eric interjected.

"Explain that," I responded. "How has the church bought into it?" Things were starting to get interesting. Somehow, the scab had been pulled off, and real feelings and perceptions were being exposed. The discussion had touched a nerve, and honest feelings and attitudes were becoming clarified.

"I thought the church was supposed to be making disciples of people, followers of Christ, not Republicans and followers of the candidate of their choosing," Eric said. "I think if people knew Jesus, they would vote right. I don't mean politically right-wing but correctly based on the character and teachings of Jesus. How did things get so far off? Many churches have become just another political institution."

"It's true," Alicia said. "Our church clearly endorses a candidate they think will get them what they want. Take abortion, for example. They think if they can get everyone to vote one way, they can get powerful laws made to stop it. Even knowing that the candidate they endorse is far from being Christ-like in character - in any way. Yet they say the end justifies the means. What the heck does that mean? Don't they believe that Jesus cares about the means? They say their candidate is the better of two evils;

therefore, he is the better candidate. What a thing to say in church! I don't think Jesus would have me vote for any evil, do you? Like these other guys, I'm fed up!" she concluded.

Holy smokes, I thought, *that was a mouthful!* I felt I had answers to what they were saying - opinions for sure – but I didn't want to interrupt what I thought the Lord was doing. These kids were thinking for themselves, seeing things the way they were, and in my opinion, they were right, believing there was a lot to fear. Yet, politics was only one of dozens of scary issues in our culture.

"What else scares you?" I asked. "I mean, other than the political climate?"

"How about the climate in general," Leah spoke out. "It's not so much the dangers we face as a species due to a rapidly changing climate; it's that we can't unite around a life-threatening crisis because of our lack of unity and polarized political views. Again, it feels like the whole human race is stuck. It makes no sense. There again, the church says it believes in the sanctity of life, but if we don't address the climate crisis, all of humanity will be in jeopardy. If we destroy the environment of the planet, we lose all life – human included."

"What really baffles me," Eric added, "is reports of the horrid disasters and the reality of climate crises are on the news nearly every day. For example, look at what just occurred in Los Angeles. They are referring to the devastating fires there as being apocalyptic. No one can deny the reality of climate change, yet so many politicians are still unwilling to pass legislation to help reverse the escalating crises. That's flat-out unbelievable when the whole planet is at stake. My great fear is what will be left of the planet when my generation wants to start families like our parents and grandparents did – It's not fair, and it's not just."

"Everybody is so short-sighted," Angie jumped in. "Everyone knows the answer to global warming is eliminating fossil fuel emissions. The pushback is all about the overuse of oil. The thing is, petroleum is a non-renewable resource. Once it's gone, it's gone forever. It's so valuable to future generations for many reasons besides being a fuel for automobiles. It's the main ingredient in plastics and synthetics; it's used in medicines and tires; it heats our homes; it's the main ingredient in paint and many other things humans need to survive. It's too important to be burned up in vehicles and omitted as toxic waste into the atmosphere. For humanity to carry on, we need it for future generations, but when it's gone, it's gone forever."

While the room tried to absorb Angie's words, Elaine quietly said, "Sorrow is another emotion I struggle with."

I almost didn't hear her. She had been sitting silent, taking in the whole conversation, but I could tell the wheels had been turning in her head. "What kind of sorrow?" I asked

All eyes turned to her. "I don't know," she came back. "I just feel sorrowful about where everything seems to be going. We all have such an unclear future with so much change going on. For one, I've been afraid to have any lasting, meaningful relationship with a man."

That caught everyone's attention. "Why is that?" Nancy asked. We were both stunned because we could see and feel her sorrow as she said it.

"If I fall in love with a man," Elaine started, "I'll naturally want to get married and start a family. To be honest, I'm afraid to have children in a world that seems so out of control and lost. Maybe I'm being silly, but it just scares me, that's all."

Nancy happened to be sitting in a chair next to her and spontaneously put her arm around her as her tears began to flow. Elaine's fear was real. Trying to talk her out of it would have been fruitless. What she needed more than anything was love, compassion, and a listening ear.

The night continued with each person openly sharing their fears and points of stress. Whether or not what they were feeling was based on reality, it was reality to them. Nancy and I knew our role was not to correct or point them back to Jesus or scripture but to listen to understand. As a pastor, it would have been a natural reaction to recite Paul's words in Philippians. "Do not be anxious about anything, but in every situation, by prayer and petition, with thanksgiving, present your requests to God. And the peace of God, which transcends all understanding, will guard your hearts and minds in Christ Jesus." But I promise you, doing that would have done more harm than good. At that moment, they needed not words or even scripture but a touch from the Spirit of God, which would become the focus of our prayer for them all.

Chapter 8 – A Flicker of Light

I can't remember the exact quote, but Martin Luther King Jr. once said something like, "It's only on the darkest night that stars can be seen." After our last meeting at the Thistle, I hoped that quote would be accurate. We had asked the question, and they had answered in total honesty. Both Nancy and I left that night with a plethora of emotions. We loved their honesty and felt privileged to have been present, but we also felt their pain and, to be honest, questioned ourselves as Christian pastors, wondering if we had been in some way guilty. We had spent most of our adult lives building a church, which had undoubtedly made some mistakes along the way without even realizing it. Even though our children no longer attended a church fellowship, we were confident they had not rejected a relationship with God. Like many parents, we asked, "Where did we go wrong – what did we do wrong?"

"One thing I wonder," Nancy said the following morning, "do you think our kids got our secondary smoke?"

I had to think for a minute about what she meant. Then, I recalled the secondary smoke analogy I had discussed with her about children exposed to the residue of their parents' cigarette smoke. At the time, I was talking about the stresses of cultural change. "What do you mean?" I asked, not understanding what she was trying to say.

"Well," she continued, "most of these kids were raised in church just like ours. I wondered if being the children of church-going parents harmed them when it came to church life?"

"But we loved church!" I reminded her. "It was our life. We had a passion for what we did. We were committed and tried to model a life of authentic Christianity. We never put on airs. How could that be negative?"

"Yes, we did love our work and were totally sincere in it, but we did have conversations they undoubtedly overheard." Nancy paused, then continued, "Much of the teaching you have done through the years has stretched people, like your commitment to creation care. You were one of the pioneers in environmental stewardship and were criticized because of it. Sometimes, people said mean things about you, and others left the church mad. Our kids were privy to many of those hurtful things and got hurt by the meanness of people, maybe more than we knew. They probably overheard a lot of our conversations. Maybe they got our secondary smoke, which poisoned their idea of the church."

I was quietly taking in all she had said. "Think of the kids we've been meeting with and their parents," I responded. "How often do kids sit in the back seats of cars going home from church or sit around the dining room table as parents criticize the Sunday message or whatever else they disagree with in their churches? I think kids naturally inherit those negative attitudes over time. Most everyone who attends church has probably been guilty of verbalizing negativity at one time or another. You're right; it's like getting secondary smoke, which can have an unhealthy lifelong impact."

"Another thing I am aware of," she said, "is how angry the group is with the Evangelical infatuation with right-wing politics. That seemed to turn them off almost more than anything else."

"I don't blame them," I said. "I'm with them on that, even though I didn't say so. Anyone who studies church history knows that reliance on the Holy Spirit diminishes when the church turns to political solutions. It's a cycle that's repeated itself over and over for the last 2000 years."

"What do you mean?" Nancy asked. "When in church history did the church become political?"

"The first time was during the time of Jesus," I answered. "That's why Jesus was so adamantly opposed to the Pharisees. They thought they could better control their culture by using legislation than by means of teaching and modeling righteousness. They hated Jesus because He believed in the separation of church and state. He saw Rome as an entity of government, saying, "Render onto Caesar what is Caesar's and unto God what is God's." The Pharisees criticized him for wanting to abolish the law, but he said he had not come to abolish it but to fulfill it. It's just that he would fulfill it through love, compassion, and mercy. He would do it a new way, His way."

I went on, "Many times, laws make everything so black and white that it takes away common sense. That was one of Sara's complaints when I first met her. Christians are meant to impact their culture by introducing people to God's heart. The Apostle Paul said that when people give their lives to Christ, they receive a 'renewal of their minds.' A true heart for God is empowered for a life of righteousness and love. When the fruits of the Holy Spirit are working in a person's life, scripture tells us there would be no need for the law."

"Sorry," I paused. "I don't mean to be preaching to you. It's just that it really bothers me when the church reverts to thinking politics is more effective than authentic Christianity."

"I can see clearly that it happened in the days of Jesus," Nancy said, "but when else did it happen?"

"The same thing happened at the Reformation," I went on. "The Catholic church wanted power over the culture and became the primary political entity in that day, even to the point of energizing and blessing the Crusades, which killed thousands upon thousands of innocent people. Then Luther preached the pure and simple gospel to young college-age students, following Jesus' model with the twelve disciples. This started another spiritual awakening that became known as the Reformation."

"Historically, this pattern repeats several more times, with the church turning away from Jesus' central words and needing a spiritual revival. John Wesley did the same thing in the 1700s when he ignited a revival known as the Great Awakening. In a lesser way, the Jesus Movement of the '60s and '70s was the same. Our generation rebelled against the establishment, the church included, and turned to the Gospel for comfort and direction."

"In a way," Nancy said, "these kids are in the same boat. I mean, they are in rebellion for much the same reason. Like all those young people from the past, they may not know it yet, but they're looking for the same thing. The authentic thing."

"I believe that's true," I said soberly. "I sure hope so. Sometimes, it feels pretty hopeless; so much damage has been done. It seems like a very dark hour for the church, with so many young people abandoning it. Yet maybe people like them will wake up, rise, and become the new flicker of light shining in a season of darkness. Maybe they will become what McKenna called the 'New Lights.'"

Chapter 9 – Encounter

It was a beautiful, warm spring day, and I was working my way along a pasture, checking for breaks in my fence line after a long, cold winter. To my surprise, I saw Shannon walking across the pasture towards me. I'll be honest. I was so enjoying the solitude that Shannon was the last person I wanted to see. In our group, he had always played the devil's advocate and was the most vocal. He was often argumentative and by far the most negative.

"Hey Shannon," I shouted, "what brings you out here on such a perfect day?"

"Thought you might like some help on the ranch," he answered.

The truth was, I didn't, but on the other hand, I'd seen something in Shannon that gave me hope. He was a rebel, and although somewhat disrespectful, he had life. One thing you couldn't say about him was that he was apathetic. He wasn't. Obnoxious, yes, but apathetic, no. Shannon had some fight in him.

"There must be some reason you'd make the drive besides wanting to stretch barbwire."

"Well," he started," I was hoping you'd be willing to talk for a few minutes without everyone else around. I have a few questions I need answers to, and they're personal." There was a softness in his voice that seemed new to me. "I know I've been kind of a pain in the ass," he stated. "It's a problem I have. I can't seem to help it, and I'm sorry. You and Nancy have given much of your time to our little group; I don't take that for granted. I know everyone really appreciates you both."

This was a different side of Shannon than I'd seen, and his countenance disarmed me. Frankly, I was taken back a bit. "What's on your mind, Shannon?" I asked. "What kind of questions?" There was a large rock not too far off, and I suggested we sit on it as the ground was still wet from spring showers.

"Questions about God," he said a bit sheepishly. "How do you know He's real? How can you be so sure?"

"Look at this place, Shannon," I started. "Look at these hills and valleys. Listen to the sounds of nature here—the birds and wind in the grass. For me, it's all a miracle. It can't be an accident or the result of happenstance."

"Yeah, I know, nature is amazing, no question. I love the out-of-doors, but what does that have to do with Jesus?" he asked.

The way he answered, I felt we were on the same page to some degree. "Are you an outdoorsman, Shannon?" I asked.

"I'm a rock climber," he said. "I'm also a mountain biker and like snowboarding in the winter. When I was young, my dad and I liked backpacking into mountain lakes and fishing. I've spent most of my life outdoors. It's where I feel the most comfortable."

"Tell me about your dad," I said. "Do you guys still spend time together?"

"No." He spoke with an edge of anger in his voice. "He and my mom got a divorce when I was fourteen. He's got a new family now. I don't see too much of him anymore."

"I'm sorry," I responded. "That's got to be hard. How about your mom?"

"My mom's great. She's the one who took me to church most of my life. I think I've disappointed her lately because I quit going, but now that I'm out of the house, I figure I can do what I want."

"You're a man now, Shannon," I affirmed. "It's time for you to make your own decisions, that's for sure. Deciding who God is in your life is a big one. I'm glad you're here."

Shannon changed the subject. "So, you seem so sure God is real, so much so you dedicated your life to telling people about Him. How can you be so sure?"

"Everyone's different, Shannon. Look at our little group at the Thistle. Talk about diversity. No two people are alike, and because of it, God meets people in different ways. I asked you about nature because that's where I found Him."

"A long time ago," Shannon continued, "I stood up in church at an altar call and said the sinner's prayer. I repeated it after the pastor. They told me I was saved and would go to heaven. I believed it for a long time, but somehow, I think it wore off. I can't say I really believe anymore, and I'm not at all sure about heaven or hell. Maybe when we die, the lights just go off."

"If it helps, Shannon, I can identify with you," I said. "I was a bit like you; I was raised in church, baptized as a child, and tried my best to be a good person. Later in life, I failed miserably. Trying to live without God is difficult. When I was about your age, I had an encounter. That's what opened my eyes and changed everything. That's what changed me forever."

"An encounter!" he exclaimed. "What the heck is an encounter? Nobody ever told me I needed an encounter. Is that even in the Bible?"

"I thought you didn't believe in the Bible," I said humorously. "It is, in a lot of cases. Like the story of Saul on the road to Damascus when God blinded him with a flash of light and spoke to him. Do you recall that?"

"Yeah, I do," he came back, "but not everyone has experiences like that."

"Not everyone asks," I said. "I did. I think some people need it more than others, and I think you're one of them."

"How do you ask for that? What do you say?"

"For me," I replied, "it took desperation. I came to a point of brokenness. My relationship with Nancy was on the line, and I had to humble myself and choose to sincerely pursue God. I know you have a hard time with the Bible because of the discrepancies you see in it. That's one reason I haven't brought up too much scripture in our small group, but bear with me for a minute. There is a scripture in the book of Romans which really spoke to me. Listen to it and tell me what you think."

"The Apostle Paul said, 'People know the truth about God because he has made it obvious to them. For ever since the world was created, people have seen the earth and sky. Through everything God made, they can clearly see his invisible qualities—his eternal power and divine nature. So, they have no excuse for not knowing God.' He is saying that man is without excuse from knowing God because he has revealed himself through His creation: His divine nature, invisible qualities, and eternal power."

"Like you," I continued, "I love nature. My whole life, I've lived in nature. I knew that if God were going to encounter me, it would be far more likely to happen in the context of nature than inside a building. Don't get me wrong, I think there is a place for the sinners' prayer you spoke of, but for me, it is more a statement of faith. My faith, however, came to me one night on a mountainside when I was all alone. I won't tell you my story now, but what happened to me on that mountain was a supernatural encounter. God revealed himself to me in a very real way as I believe He wants to do for you."

Shannon was trying to digest what I'd said before he spoke. "That's okay for people like you and me, but what about so many of my friends who hardly ever get outside? Most of them waste their time playing video games and are addicted to social media. How can they ever have this encounter you're talking about?"

"First of all," I said, "I feel sorry for them, but there are many pathways that lead to the discovery of God. Some people discover Him through the arts: poetry, music, sculpture, and graphic arts. Some discover him through a season of desperation and brokenness. Some find him through acts of mercy and compassion, while others find him through intellectual study and religious ritual. God is creative, and because He has created everyone differently, He has provided many ways for people to discover His love for them. For me, it was through nature."

"By the way," I continued, "I discovered each part of the Trinity (Father, Son, and Holy Spirit) at different times, all with supernatural encounters in the context of nature."

"That's a lot to digest," Shannon said. "Where should I begin?"

"With hunger," I responded. "Shannon, you've got to want it. You've got to see your need for it. You wouldn't have made this drive today if you didn't care. I know you care, and further, I know God cares. He wants you. He not only wants you but has a plan for you."

"I've always sort of felt that," Shannon said, "but if that's the case, why did my parents divorce, and why did my dad abandon us? Sometimes I think my life was an accident, that I was never really wanted."

"Listen to me, Shannon, if God didn't want you, you wouldn't be on this earth. And because He did want you, He has a reason for you to be here, not just here, but here right now. The Bible tells us that when we give our lives to him as an act of worship, he will reveal His good, pleasing, and perfect will for us. That's where this is all going. God has more in store for you than you can imagine."

Shannon helped me mend the fence for a while, but it was clear he had come for a more significant reason. That day, I saw a different side to him, and it endeared him to me. I no longer just tolerated him being in our group but sincerely cared for his future. Later that day, I found Nancy in her garden pulling weeds. I shared with her what had happened, and together, we prayed that Shannon would have an authentic encounter with God soon.

Chapter 10 – A Turning Point

The evenings were getting warmer, which made our meetings at The Dusty Thistle somewhat more comfortable. Brad continued to be a great host to the young folks. The group had begun to grow as the word started to leak out among their friends. As a result, our level of intimacy began to change, not for the worse, but it was different. I thought the change was a good thing. I believed we needed to change if the meetings were to continue successfully. There had been no intention for the group to grow into some form of church; that had never been our intention. Nancy and I began to feel that our time with them at The Dusty Thistle was ending. For several months, we listened to and affirmed this small group of young people we had grown to love, but we knew their future, whatever it would become, had to be their choice.

During earlier gatherings, when people were still expressing their feelings, we learned that Paul, who had been with us from the beginning, was a musician. He played several instruments but showed up with a guitar that night. To our surprise, Leah, also a musician, showed up with a violin, which was also unannounced. Brad had opened his bar, and people were taking him up on his offer for refreshments. After chatting and laughing, we all pulled up chairs, forming them into a circle as before, but now it had become noticeably larger.

"Paul, you brought your guitar," I commented. "And Leah—you brought your violin," I said the obvious, but I thought it needed to be acknowledged. "What's the plan?"

I asked what the plan was because we never had one. Spontaneity had been how we had been operating from the beginning, and I didn't want it to stop. Nancy and I loved that we were not in charge of the group. We had birthed it with the idea of letting it become whatever the Lord wanted it to be.

Sara, the original instigator of our gatherings, had become the unofficial leader of the meetings, and everyone's eyes gravitated toward her.

She looked a little sheepish, not seeing herself in such a position, but realized everyone there responded to her as the facilitator. "Can you guys play together?" she asked.

Leah spoke first, "I can follow almost any instrument," she said, "but it was Paul's idea to show up with a little music." She looked at Paul for a response.

"Earlier," he began, "during our first meetings here at the Thistle, I complained about what some churches refer to as worship, which is a time of singing before the announcements and the sermon gets started. I shared how I felt there needed to be a change in that part of church services because it had become a predictable thirty-to-forty-minute event with songs that required PowerPoint slides for people to participate. I also shared how nearly all the churches I attended followed the same format. I can't say what is right or wrong; I just know what ministers to me. Because of my sharing, I later felt guilty about my negativity, thinking if I wanted change, I should be a part of it. Over the past weeks, I've been working on some simple songs I wanted to share with you guys."

With that, Paul started strumming his guitar with his eyes closed, and Leah softly followed his lead. As Paul started singing, Nancy and I knew something sacred was beginning to happen. Both of our eyes began filling with tears. We felt the Spirit of God like we hadn't for a long time. Neither of us could explain it, but we knew something powerful was happening.

Paul sang a stanza of simple but heartfelt lyrics. His words expressed what the Lord had been doing in his heart, resonating with the feeling of nearly everyone present. As he began repeating the simple lyrics, the entire room joined him. It was simple but so pure and relevant to what everyone was experiencing and feeling. For the first time, it was like our group, who had been so antagonistic and broken, were embracing and returning to their love for the Lord. We sang the stanza repeatedly until Paul and Leah brought it to a gentle and solemn close. The room was silent, and God's presence was tangible. Someone started to pray, thanking God for His presence, and the sound of weeping could be heard. Nancy and I were a mess ourselves because what had happened was clearly a result of the presence of God, and it stirred in us a remembrance from years past.

Sara broke the silence. Looking at Nancy and me, she said, "I don't know if this is the Lord telling me this, but I was wondering if you guys would share your experience during the early days of your faith. We've all heard of the Jesus Movement, but obviously, none of us can fully understand it. It's ancient history to us, but seeing your reaction to Paul and Leah's song, I felt there is something deep and special for us to understand."

Nancy and I were a little undone and couldn't fully comprehend why. Nancy looked at me and asked, "Do you remember that night, years ago, in our old cabin at the ranch, when a group of our friends showed up, and we sat around the small living room? Those were the days before we had electricity; the only lights we had were gas lights and lanterns, which hissed. Our friend Debbie Springer showed up unannounced with her guitar, much like Paul did tonight. None of us had any experience with small group worship, but she started playing that simple old song, 'I love you, Lord.' Do you remember that?"

"I do, " I said. "Like tonight, it was magical. It unexpectedly slammed us all." Then I spontaneously recited the simple lyrics: "I love you, Lord, and I lift my voice to worship you. Oh, my soul, rejoice."

"Yes," Nancy said, "and we sang from our hearts for the first time. In some ways, that was our first real experience with true worship. We were never the same again after that. We couldn't get enough of it."

"What got you guys started in the Jesus Movement?" Sara asked. "Did you go to it, or did it come to you?"

"Nancy and I were in our mid-20s, just like you guys," I answered. "We were hungry for something real. We were raised in church, but it had become irrelevant to our generation."

"Just like us!" Eric jumped in.

"Much the same," I came back. "Even the times were similar. Our generation had just emerged from the '60s rebellion, and the established church didn't seem relevant to us. Like you, we were stirred up and anxious about our uncertain future. We were afraid of the rapid changes going on in our society and needed something to anchor us. We wanted the truth because our government had been untruthful. We were in the aftermath of the Vietnam War and a government scandal called Watergate. Most of our generation was checking out emotionally, some using drugs, and some breaking down traditional social norms, especially in the areas of love and sex. The singers of our time, like Bob Dylan and Simon and Garfunkel, were singing lyrics that were prophetic in a way. Much of their music spoke of what we were feeling. When the Jesus Movement emerged, that style of music merged into our gatherings. The churches we once had attended sang out of hymnals and with choirs. None of that transferred over in this new move of God."

"Where were you meeting?" one of the others asked.

"Like you, we were a poor bunch. We were young; many were starting a professional life with low incomes. In Nancy's and my case, we were starting a family. None of us had the resources to help financially, so we met in schools or warehouses. Not only that, but we did things in non-religious ways on purpose to make statements that we had rejected the churches of our parents. We had the statement, 'We don't put money into bricks and mortar but into ministry.' We wouldn't baptize in the building but only in natural settings like the ocean or rivers because we wanted everything to be unorthodox."

"Like The Dusty Thistle!" someone interjected.

"In a way, yes. Only we were a little more legalistic than you guys; we would have never met in a pub." Everyone laughed, especially Brad, who stood, as usual, behind the bar.

"The point is," I said with a fresh sense of revelation, "what happened to us is almost exactly what's happening to you, except what you're facing is like being on steroids compared to what we faced."

"How so?" Shannon asked.

"Our generation birthed what was called the drug revolution by using a weak strain of marijuana and hallucinogenic drugs like LSD. Your generation is dealing with opioids and other drugs that are killing thousands. Our generation feared the coming environmental condition of the earth. We recognized that the world would be heating up; we called it the Greenhouse Effect and feared it. You guys are living amid the reality of the acceleration of climate change. We feared a growing world population that would demand more food, water, and space than the world could provide. The world's population doubled in our lifetime from about 2.5 billion to 5 billion, and we were still only in our early twenties. Books like *The Population Bomb* scared us, saying the world could not be sustainable after it hit 8 billion. Today, the world has passed the eight billion mark. It is beginning to suffer the consequences with mass migrations of desperate people, food and water pollution, the acceleration of climate change, and the threat of global war."

"Whatever happened to the Jesus Movement? What happened to all those who experienced it?" Alicia spoke up. "I mean, you guys are here and still following God, but how about all the others?"

"The Jesus Movement wasn't what we call a real 'Awakening'. It was a revival, no doubt, but like many revivals, it lost its momentum in the 1980s. It birthed churches like Calvary Chapel and Vineyard Christian Fellowship, which are still alive and well today, but even those movements slowed way down."

"Why?" Shannon blurted out emotionally. "What happened to all those people?"

"Two things I can think of offhand," I replied. "The first was a cultural shift called the Yuppies."

"Yuppies? What's that?" someone spoke.

"A young, educated, rich person," I answered. "They were people in our generation who sold out to the establishment. Yuppie is slang referring to a young, educated person who lives in a city, is successful in business, and has a lifestyle involving spending a lot of money. Money has a way of changing people," I said. "I wish it weren't true, but it is. Many of these people stayed cultural Christians but attended rich megachurches that preached prosperity messages."

"There is a scripture in the book of Proverbs that says it best as a prayer: Give me neither poverty nor riches but give me only my daily bread. Otherwise, I may have too much and disown you and say, 'Who is the Lord? Or I may become poor and steal, and so dishonor the name of my God." [Proverbs 30:9]

"What's the second thing?" Shannon asked.

"Politics," I said.

There was a gasp in the room. "Politics took the wind out of the Jesus Movement?" someone asked but said it more as a statement than a question.

"Yes, politics," I restated. "Explaining what happened might take a minute, but I'm willing to share what I know if you guys are willing to listen."

Several spoke at the same time, "We are."

Then Elaine added, "Boy, some things just won't ever change. Why can't people learn?"

"This may sound like a history lesson," I said, "but here's what happened. During the 1980s, something emerged that nobody thought a lot about at the time. Jerry Falwell Sr., a Southern Baptist pastor who had become well-known in the televangelist world, founded the 'Moral Majority.' Falwell rejected the Southern Baptist conviction for separating church and state. He believed America should be a Christian nation, believing freedom of religion was meant to apply to Christianity only. He rallied Christians across the country to fight to keep prayer in public schools, which most church leaders accepted as a righteous cause and promoted as well. He believed America was a nation of traditional family values and spoke out against homosexuality, abortion, feminism, and other forms of what he called social and moral decay. He joined forces with other highly influential leaders like Pat Robertson of the Christian Coalition and leaders of the Religious Right. Together, they became a changing force of direction within most Evangelical and some Catholic circles. The Religious Right had three objectives: One, to get conservative Evangelicals to participate in the political process. Two, to draw them into the Republican Party, and three, to elect social conservatives into public office. Their objective was not to merely connect the church with the state, but to dominate and control it."

"I don't want to interrupt," Sara broke in, "but the values they decided to fight for were their own. I mean, Jesus said very little or nothing about any of them specifically. You would have thought they would have chosen the things Jesus was most passionate about. Things like caring for the poor, the hungry, the sick, the prisoner, the immigrant; Jesus said his main objective was to set the captives free and heal the brokenhearted."

"I agree," I said, "but at the time, those of us who were leaders in the church couldn't fully comprehend how much this movement would redirect the Evangelical Christian faith and how far off base it would take the people we were called to lead. Looking back, I think we weren't paying attention. I personally did not like televangelists. I didn't like how they raised vast amounts of money from well-meaning people. I hated the fanfare and the hype, but I didn't realize how much they were changing the complexion of the church in general and how contrary much of their message was to the heart of Jesus. Although they never said it outright, the overriding message was, 'We, the Church, haven't been able to change American culture with prayer or by teaching the simple Gospel, so we must turn to politics to get what we want.' It was the same message the Pharisees taught during the days of Jesus. They, too, attempted to control the culture of their day through the law, which was diametrically opposed to the message of Jesus, who believed actual change would only come through changed hearts."

"Wow!" Sara responded. "I have never heard any of that. Those guys undermined the amazing thing God was trying to do in your generation. It's just so sad, but it explains why Evangelicals are where they are today. Funny thing, people like my parents don't even know what happened to them. They had the Spirit of God sucked right out of their churches. No wonder our generation is leaving church in droves."

"Maybe it's not a bad thing," I spoke. "New wineskins have never come along in good times. The old order must die before God will birth something new and fresh. You guys are a part of what He's doing in your generation."

The room fell quiet for quite a while until Shannon spoke. "We need to ponder these things for a while before we react. I'm afraid I might start saying stuff I'll regret. I, for one, need time to think and sort this out. I believe we have some choices to make – all of us."

Chapter 11 – What Is It You Want?

Spring had arrived on our mountain, and the warmth of the morning sun beckoned Nancy and me to leave the ranch house and enjoy the smells and sounds of the countryside. Wolfie, our young shepherd dog, and his half-sister Sadie were also raring to go. They liked nothing better than being with the two of us on our outdoor excursions. New growth was shooting up everywhere, and wildflowers were blooming on the south-facing slopes of the ravines.

As it often was these days, much of our conversation centered around our experiences at The Dusty Thistle with this growing bunch of young people. Every meeting was different, but each one had taught us things we could have never guessed. It was one of the highlights of our thirty-five years of full-time ministry. I had just turned seventy-seven years old and was starting to feel my age, wondering if the Lord was done using me when my first encounter with Sara gave me a new purpose. It had been an incredible six months, meeting every other week with this special bunch of kids. We recalled that we already had two children and a sense of direction for our lives when we were their age. That was something this group was coming to. Most were still single, yet two young married couples had recently joined us.

"I feel like our time at the Thistle is ending," I told Nancy. "It's been a rich time, but I think they need to discover a fresh way to carry on these conversations. When we first started, I thought this experience was more about deconstruction than reconstruction, but in the last month, things have shifted."

"I agree with the idea that our time is concluding," she said, "but explain what you mean by reconstruction."

I knew what I had said needed an explanation, so I began, "Based on what Sara shared when we first spoke with her about her friends, I thought these kids were done with Christianity altogether, but it wasn't Christianity they struggled with so much as their church experience. They don't want to deconstruct their faith as much as reconstruct how they express it. According to most Christian sociologists I've read, 'deconstruction' is giving up the Christian faith to find another form of spirituality. Many end up making up their own belief system."

"That would be so unfortunate," Nancy said. "It's sad how the basics of the Christian faith and the heart of Jesus get so muddled and misunderstood. I know our role hasn't been to preach or teach but to provide a listening ear, but frequently, they have looked to us for answers."

I paused and then answered, "Well, lately, they have been asking for our input and perspective, and I feel if they ask, we should be honest and tell them what we think. They have especially been interested in our experiences and journey with the Lord."

"Yes," she replied," like in our last meeting. Your question to them really broke something open. Had we not been a part of this experience, that might not have ever happened. They have needed our guidance up until now."

"Do you mean when I asked them to define what they wanted?"

"Yes," she said again. But your question was more than that. For weeks, they have told us what they didn't want and didn't like, but when you asked them what it was they really wanted, it changed everything. It stopped them thinking in the negative long enough to ponder their lives."

"It did have a different effect for sure," I said. "When I clarified the question, telling them to think about what they really want in their hearts. What did they want out of life? What would they be willing to ask the Lord for?"

"I loved hearing Shannon say that he wanted more than anything to have an encounter with the Lord," she continued. "What a change it was to see his eyes fill up with tears and his words become soft and sincere. I believe it is what he wants. Then, Sherri and Dan, shared how much they had been praying to have a child and how difficult it had been to get pregnant. They were so vulnerable and fragile."

"We've turned a corner this past month," I agreed. "There was tenderness and openness that hadn't been there earlier. Like when Alicia shared about the riff that had opened with her family because she began questioning her faith and her reasons for leaving the church. She was broken and wanted them to understand and let her be her own person. That was a tough one."

"Her questioning challenged them in a way they hadn't been challenged before," Nancy said. "Her perceptions of her family's charismatic / Pentecostal church style were impressive. She didn't deny the reality of the Holy Spirit but had a hard time with the theology and methodology in their church life and how contrary it was to their daily life. She saw excessiveness and, in a way, hypocrisy. It's what we used to call 'name it and claim it.' You and I have seen God genuinely and miraculously heal and set people free, but we've also seen people claim things that aren't true. I never want to get tired of praying for the sick, but I will always want it to be genuine, and I believe that's what she wanted."

"A lot of what these young folks want is the genuine article," I reflected.

"It's what we always wanted, too," Nancy concluded.

We walked a while, keeping to our own thoughts. The dogs were everywhere, sniffing and digging up gophers and squirrels who constantly outsmarted them. It was hard to know who was harassing who. We crossed a small, babbling creek and sat in the sunshine on a grassy south slope. "There's one thing I'd like to ask them," I spoke, breaking the silence. "It's something I've wondered for a long time. I don't think they'd have the answer, but I'd like to hear their thoughts anyway."

"I give up," Nancy replied, "tell me. Our next meeting may be our last, so you better ask whatever it is."

"Nobody could have ever predicted or guessed what the church would look like after the Jesus Movement started. I don't think anyone ever thought about it. It just took on a form over time. It just evolved into something very different than the Body of Christ had seen before. The funny thing is, one of the issues these kids are complaining about is that all the churches they have attended have a predicable format or feel: thirty minutes of worship led by a worship band, announcements, forty minutes of exegetical teaching, and maybe some Spirit-filled ministry or an altar-call depending on the church. That's exactly the format of the first Calvary and Vineyard churches born in the 1970s. Now, over 50 years later, it's still the same thing, just a lot more professional and, in some ways, with less Spirit-filled activity. In those days, we longed to be like the New Testament church, embracing and practicing the gifts of the Holy Spirit. Sometimes, it's hard to remember back that far, but I recall how our worship times were filled with wonder."

"I remember it, too," Nancy said with a hint of sorrow. "We were encouraged from the beginning to keep our eyes closed during our worship times to better experience God's presence without distraction. It was easy to do because the lyrics were so familiar and simple. We never had song sheets and overhead projectors weren't widespread. The songs in those days had men's and women's parts as we would sometimes echo each other. I also remember getting lost in the music. The entire congregation often broke into times of singing in tongues, or at different times, someone would begin singing what we called the Song of the Lord, which was a form of singing prophetic lyrics to the melodies. It was normal practice but slowly faded from our church culture over time. Some said it disturbed the visitors who came to experience our services. It was unique to that day and very different from anything we had experienced in the traditional churches we had grown up in, that's for sure. It was a new wineskin that influenced churches for a long time."

We sat quietly for a while, reflecting on our past journey. Nancy interrupted our reverie by asking, "So, what's the question you wanted to ask them?"

"Oh yeah," I said. "Here is the question for which I'd love to have an answer: If there is to be an awakening or at least a revival of young people, what would a fresh move of God look like in today's culture? What form would it take? Not just the church buildings, if there were any, but the whole style of church life. When it happened in our generation, we moved from steepled church buildings to gymnasiums and warehouses; we rejected formal choirs and made the entire church body the choir. Stuff like that was radical in our day, but now it's just another old wineskin. I want to get their impressions or thoughts on the kind of ministry they would be drawn to. It's a continuation of the question, 'What do you really want?'"

Chapter 12 – Deconstruction? / Reconstruction?

Nancy and I could sense a change in the atmosphere as we entered The Dusty Thistle. It was a beautiful late spring evening. Although the warmer days allowed the rollup door (a remnant from the building's previous days as a workshop) to be open, the larger parlor stove was ablaze, creating the cozy atmosphere we were accustomed to. Brad's bar was open, and many of the crowd were standing around holding glasses or bottles, depending on their choice of beverage. Everything seemed pretty much as usual, except for an emotional sobriety we couldn't account for. Once again, the group had grown a little as the word had spread. The Dusty Thistle had become a special place to be.

After some time, we circled the chairs and barstools, and people introduced the new friends they had invited. Many knew this might be

Nancy's and my last evening with them. Nobody knew for sure where things would be headed after this night, creating a sense of uncertainty. Paul began strumming his guitar with Leah following him on her violin. He sang a new song, which we were all inclined to listen to rather than participate in. Without being told, we sensed that this song contained a message; its lyrics told a compelling story of our growing time together. When he was done, the room fell silent until some spontaneous prayer expressed the gratitude and thanksgiving we were all feeling.

Nancy spoke up and told everyone how our time with them had been an incredible privilege and honor. She thanked them for letting us be a part of their journeys and told them I had a favor to ask this last evening.

"What?" Sara asked. "What kind of favor?"

"Just another question," I replied. "It's a continuation of the question I asked two weeks ago, but I'm not sure if any of us have an answer to it."

"What question?" Alicia answered. "I don't think you could ask anything Shannon wouldn't think he has an answer to," she said jokingly, and the room broke out in laughter. Shannon had clearly gained a reputation.

I began, "Two weeks ago, I asked what you want, and more specifically, tonight, I am asking, what are you looking for? When it comes to church, all of you have expressed what you don't want, but tonight, let's talk about what you do want."

"About eight years ago," I continued, "I wrote *Re:Form – The Decline of American Evangelicalism and a Path for the New Generation to ReForm their Faith*. Maybe because of this book, I have loved being with you these last months. In it, I predicted a mass exit of the Millennial generation from the Christian church and some from the Christian faith. I also predicted their generation would rediscover a new kind of Christianity, much like my generation did in the '60s and '70s, but that didn't happen. Now, my hope is for Gen Z, your generation. The question I have concerns what a new form of Christianity might look like if there would be a revival in your generation?"

Again, the room was quiet. I could see wheels turning in everyone's heads. "A couple of days ago, Nancy and I were on a walk," I informed them, "and we talked about this. We reflected on our involvement in the Jesus Movement and how much the new churches differed from anything before, mainly the traditional mainline protestant and Catholic churches. Our new move of God took on a whole different form and look. My question is simply this: what would it look like if there was a breakout of revival in your generation?"

"How would we know that?" Eric asked. "You just said yourself, you couldn't have guessed how your church experience would look after the Jesus Movement took root. How could we?"

"You couldn't," I responded. "So, I guess the question is, if any of you were to start attending church again, and I'm not saying you will, what characteristics would have to be present there? In other words, what would you be looking for?"

"Love and kindness!" Elaine exclaimed. "Unconditional love, acceptance, and no judgment. It would have to be a place anyone could come to and feel comfortable: gender, race, color, sexual identity, everything. Everyone would be accepted and loved without judgment or prejudice. Jesus said it was the first and most important commandment, and His kingdom was based on it."

Heads nodded in affirmation to what Elaine said, and again, the room went silent.

Paul said, "Many churches say, 'Come as you are, you'll be loved.' But the underlying message is, then you can repent, change, and fall into our definition of righteousness."

I had to silently laugh because, years before, as a pastor, I had bumper stickers made that said that just that. What he said concerning the underlying message was the very thing I had believed. Right or wrong, I felt a little busted.

"If you're making a list," Sara said, "add compassion, justice, and mercy. My favorite verse in the Old Testament is Micah 6:8: And what does the Lord require of you? To act justly and to love mercy and to walk humbly with your God. It's true, I'd agree with Elaine; love and kindness are the foundation, but compassion for this broken world and all the broken people in it is an expression of love. If I were to be a part of a church again, it would be to participate in ministries that show compassion and justice. There would have to be active ministries and opportunities to feed and clothe the poor. One thing I've contemplated doing is going south and walking with those thousands of immigrants who are trying to find justice in America because there is none in their home countries. For that reason, I've been learning to speak Spanish, and it would be my idea of active, authentic Christianity."

"Okay," Shannon broke in, "what I'd like would be a fellowship of believers, call it church if you want, modeled after the church in the Book of Acts. Those people were serious about their faith and felt it necessary to be around others who shared their convictions. They were, as it said, 'of one heart and one mind.' They shared everything so no one would have need."

"Sounds like socialism," said Eric.

"Socialism! What do you mean socialism?" Shannon retorted. "They weren't communists."

"First of all," Eric said to clarify, "socialism is far from communism. They aren't at all the same thing. The book of Acts describes the church's activity in several places." He opened a Bible he had brought, which was unusual for this group, and read two passages. "Acts chapter two says that right after the first church was formed, 'All the believers were together and had everything in common. They sold property and possessions to give to anyone who had need.' Acts four said, 'All the believers were one in heart and mind. No one claimed that any of their possessions was their own, but they shared everything they had. With great power the apostles continued to testify to the resurrection of the Lord Jesus. And God's grace was so powerfully at work in them all that there were no needy persons among them. For from time to time those who owned land or houses sold them, brought the money from the sales and put it at the apostles' feet, and it was distributed to anyone who had need.'

"I'm not saying it's bad," Eric continued. "I agree with you that it's the way the church should work, but most conservatives in our country would accuse a church like that of being socialistic. They might even have to call Jesus a socialist if you read what he said about separating the sheep and goats in Matthew 25. For Him, it was all about the hungry, the thirsty, the prisoner, and caring for the poor in general."

Suddenly, I started thinking how fascinating the conversation was getting. I loved that they were not only thinking but, for the first time, reading scripture to one another to express what Christianity was about. They started to see what a radical book it was and how much, especially the words of Jesus, resonated with their personal desires.

"For me," Alicia said, "the message would have to be open and honest regarding the present-day culture. As we've already said, it couldn't be politically biased. Still, we would have to be fearless and point out the issues of world crises and injustice, not tiptoeing around sensitive issues for the sake of not losing people. In fact, it should not make the size of the congregation the definition or goal for success. The church should be a place that teaches and models godliness, character, and integrity."

"Another thing," Paul added, "as it has in centuries past, the church should be a champion for music and the arts. It should be an expression of creativity. God is a creative God who has created us in his image; He's put creativity into our DNA. That would be important to me."

"All of that is fine and good," Leah said, "but don't you think we're missing something? I do. I think we are missing the most important thing. How about the authentic presence of God? Isn't that really what we want more than anything? My heart ached when Nancy shared how they had tasted and experienced God's grace and how it was the glue that kept them coming back to church as young people. I deeply desire what she experienced: the authentic presence of God and the power of the Holy Spirit working among my generation. I've heard pastors claim from their pulpits that God was present and active in their service, but I couldn't feel anything. I don't want to be critical, I really don't, but I need this for myself. I need to know and experience God's presence for myself. I need an encounter with God. A firsthand experience."

"As I've already confessed," Shannon continued, "I want an encounter with God, too." Then he turned his gaze on me. "You told me God wouldn't have put me on this earth if He didn't love and want me. You told me I wasn't an accident, no matter how I was conceived. You told me that God wanted me and had a purpose for my life. If I knew what that was, I'd serve Him for the rest of my life. I want what Leah says she wants, and if it happens, I'll be shouting it from the rooftops."

"And if you do, Shannon," I interjected, "thousands of young people will listen and follow."

"The question I have," Leah broke in, "is where can we go if we decide to give Christianity a second chance? Where can we find a church that fills all these criteria?"

"I'm sure there are some," I said. "I know there are thousands of humble, Christ-centered pastors who desire what you want. The answer to this isn't trying another gimmick or program. The answer is for God to break into a hungry generation and provide a ministry that He ordains. A ministry that understands your generation and is willing to change everything if necessary to address it head-on. But, if you can't find it in the established church, my council is for you to start it yourself. During the Jesus Movement, we had a few older, seasoned leaders willing to change everything they were doing, but many churches that exploded across the country were led by people your age. Most pastors were in their 20s or early 30s. Maybe it is for you to do."

The conversation grew in intensity and carried on late into the evening. They told me the church would have to openly address what they feared and were anxious about, subjects like the global environment, climate change, and the future of water and food. It wouldn't just address these issues but provide ministries where people could serve. Ministries that would focus on the real issues without apology. People in their generation would like to believe they could make a difference in the world, and a church that provides opportunities in ministry to seriously engage in the crisis would, I believe, be sought after.

I was pleased with their thinking and responses. They were a good bunch, and I knew Nancy and I would miss meeting with them. Yet I also knew we had come to a point of decision, a fork in the road: deconstruction going one way and reconstruction going another. It would be up to them which fork they would choose. Our prayer, of course, would be that they would all take the right turn.

The final thing we did for them on that last evening was to pray for them. We used the prayer Paul had prayed 2000 years ago over the Ephesian church:

"For this reason, I kneel before the Father, from whom every family in heaven and on earth derives its name. I pray that out of his glorious riches he may strengthen you with power through his Spirit in your inner being, so that Christ may dwell in your hearts through faith. And I pray that you, being rooted and established in love, may have power, together with all the Lord's holy people, to grasp how wide and long and high and deep is the love of Christ, and to know this love that surpasses knowledge—that you may be filled to the measure of all the fullness of God."

We all learned a tremendous amount during those months at the Dusty Thistle. Nancy and I had pastored a large church for 25 years, but based on what we had heard over the last six months, we felt convicted on a number of points. We knew if we had a second chance after what we had experienced, we would have done many things differently. At this point, it was water under the bridge for us, but we could only pray newer, younger pastors and leaders, both men and women, would rise in this moment of crisis and opportunity. Rise to hear the cries of their generation, discern right from wrong, see through the criticism and anger, and build churches for a fresh new season of

Christianity. We prayed this generation would have the opportunity to experience what we had experienced when we were their age. With everything in us, we believed the time and culture were ripe for a fresh new harvest. After our time with this handful of young people, we believed God had been preparing a new breed of courageous young leaders who would seize the moment, as did the Luthers, the Wesleys, and many others. Those men and women of the past understood the times in which they lived and knew what to do about it.

Other than having a willing and listening ear, Nancy and I realized there was little more we could contribute. We knew we had long ago lost the energy required to take a role in what might come. Our role now was to fervently pray this small group would choose the path of reconstruction over deconstruction, returning to the roots of their Christian faith. And, by God's grace, they might discover and participate in birthing a fresh new expression of that faith. This expression could break open a new door, inviting an authentic spiritual awakening for their generation.

Oh Lord, please let it be.

www.ingramcontent.com/pod-product-compliance
Lightning Source LLC
Chambersburg PA
CBHW060617080526
44585CB00013B/865